KUDUS

FOOTBALL AND LIFE

Inside the World of True Fans

By Pitt Anddy

© Copyright 2024 - All rights reserved.

No part of this book may be copied, reproduced, or transmitted without express written consent from the publisher or the author. There shall be no legal or moral liability placed on the publisher or author for any losses, liabilities, or financial harm resulting directly or indirectly from the material in this book. You are in charge of your own decisions, deeds, and outcomes.

Legal Disclaimer: This book is copyrighted. This book is strictly for personal use only. Without the author's or publisher's permission, you may not change, distribute, sell, use, quote, or paraphrase any of the content in this book.

Disclaimer Notice: Please note the information contained within this document is for educational and entertainment purposes only. All effort has been executed to present accurate, up to date, and reliable, complete information. No warranties of any kind are declared or implied. Readers acknowledge that the author is not engaging in the rendering of legal, financial, medical, or professional advice.

The content within this book has been derived from various sources. Please consulta licensed professional before attempting any techniques outlined in this book. By reading this document, the reader agrees that under no circumstances is the author responsible for any losses, direct or indirect, which are incurred as a result of the use of the information contained within this document, including, but not limited to, errors, omissions, or inaccuracies.

INTRODUCTION

Discover the motivational tale of Mohammed Kudus, the master of West Ham's midfield, by watching "Kudus – Football And Life". This well-researched and fascinating book explores the life and career of the Ghanaian midfield player, following his remarkable rise from a bright young player to a pivotal role in a highly competitive league in Europe.

Readers will find lesser-known tales, crucial exchanges, and seminal moments that have shaped Kudus's development on both a personal and professional level within these pages. His early years playing football in Ghana are chronicled in the book, along with his smooth transition to the Premier League and the qualities that have made him an invaluable member of West Ham's team.

"Kudus – Football And Life" provides a close-up view of the player's journey via in-depth interviews, eye-catching graphics, and thorough analysis. Ideal for passionate supporters and football aficionados, this book offers an in-depth analysis of a crucial midfield player for West Ham.

Explore Kudus's philosophy of football, his tactical acumen, and the goals that propel him to succeed on the field. "Kudus – Football And Life" honors his incredible career, which had a profound effect on West Ham and the football community at large.

TABLE OF CONTENTS

INTRODUCTION 4

PERSONAL LIFE 7

CLUB CAREER 19

NATIONAL TEAM CAREER 31

RECORDS AND PERSONAL
ACHIEVEMENTS 42

TECHNIQUE AND PLAYING STYLE 50

PERSONAL LIFE

- Early Life: Mohammed Kudus was born on 2 August 2000 in Nima, a densely populated neighbourhood in Accra, Ghana. His upbringing in this challenging environment shaped his character and resilience.
- Boyhood Club: Kudus began his football journey with Strong Tower FC, a local club in Nima. His early

performances at Kawukudi Park showcased his talent and passion for the sport.

⚽   Family Support: Kudus comes from a close-knit family. His uncle, Abdul Fatawu Alhassan, often speaks about how proud the family is of his achievements and his role as a torchbearer for Nima.

⚽   Educational Balance: Kudus balanced his football

training with education. He attended school while playing for Strong Tower FC, demonstrating his commitment to both academics and football.

⚽ Right to Dream Academy: At the age of 12, Kudus joined the Right to Dream Academy in Akosombo, Ghana. This academy played a crucial role in his development, providing both football training and education.

- ⚽ Nickname "World's Best": His coach at Strong Tower FC, Joshua 'Ayoba' Awuah, nicknamed him "World's Best" due to his exceptional skills and potential at a young age.
- ⚽ Community Role Model: Kudus is considered a role model in Nima. His success story inspires many young

people in the community to pursue their dreams despite the challenges they face.

- ⚽ Philanthropy: Kudus frequently returns to Nima to donate football boots and other equipment to his boyhood club and young aspiring footballers, giving back to the community that supported him.
- ⚽ Multilingual: During his football career in various

countries, Kudus has picked up multiple languages, including English and Dutch, enhancing his communication skills on and off the pitch.

⚽   Cultural Ambassador: Kudus is proud of his Ghanaian heritage and often speaks about how his culture influences his life and career. He serves as a cultural ambassador for Ghana wherever he goes.

⚽ Favourite Player: Kudus idolised Brazilian footballer Ronaldinho growing up. He often tried to emulate Ronaldinho's flair and creativity on the pitch.

⚽ Strong Character: Those who know Kudus describe him as having a strong character and a relentless work ethic. His determination and attitude have been key to his success.

- ⚽ International Recognition: Kudus's performances have earned him recognition beyond Ghana. He was nominated for the prestigious Golden Boy Award by Italy's Tuttosport newspaper in 2020.
- ⚽ Injury Resilience: Despite facing several injuries early in his career, Kudus has shown

remarkable resilience and determination to bounce back and perform at the highest level.

- Personal Motto: Kudus lives by the motto "Stay humble and work hard." This philosophy reflects in his approach to both his personal life and professional career.
- Humility: Friends and family describe Kudus as humble despite his success.

He remains grounded and maintains a strong connection with his roots in Nima.

- ⚽ Role in National Team: Kudus scored on his international debut for Ghana against South Africa in a 2021 AFCON qualifier, marking his arrival on the international stage.
- ⚽ Community Engagement: Beyond football, Kudus is

involved in various community initiatives aimed at supporting underprivileged children and promoting education through sports.

- Mentorship: Kudus often mentors young footballers in Ghana, sharing his experiences and offering guidance to help them navigate their football careers.

⚽ Media Presence: Kudus is active on social media, where he shares glimpses of his life, training, and matches. He uses his platform to connect with fans and inspire the next generation.

CLUB CAREER

- Youth Development at Right to Dream Academy: Mohammed Kudus began his football journey at the Right to Dream Academy in Ghana, where he honed his skills from 2012 to 2018.
- Professional Debut at FC Nordsjaelland: Kudus made his professional debut for Danish club FC Nordsjaelland on 5 August 2018, shortly after

his 18th birthday. He quickly established himself as a key player.

- First Professional Goal: He scored his first professional goal on 4 March 2019 in a Superliga match against Randers FC, helping his team secure a 2-1 victory.
- Breakthrough Season: Kudus had a standout season in 2019-2020, scoring 11 goals in 25 league appearances for

FC Nordsjaelland. His performances attracted interest from top European clubs.

- Transfer to Ajax: In July 2020, Kudus signed with Dutch giants Ajax for a reported fee of €9 million. This move marked a significant step in his career, joining one of Europe's top clubs.

- ⚽ Ajax Debut: Kudus made his debut for Ajax on 20 September 2020 in an Eredivisie match against RKC Waalwijk, where he provided an assist in a 3-0 win.
- ⚽ First Ajax Goal: He scored his first goal for Ajax on 3 October 2020 in a 5-1 victory over SC Heerenveen, showcasing his scoring ability early in his tenure with the club.

- ⚽ Injury Setbacks: Despite a promising start at Ajax, Kudus faced injury setbacks during his first season, including a knee injury that sidelined him for several months.
- ⚽ Eredivisie Champion: Kudus played a part in Ajax's 2020-2021 Eredivisie title win, contributing with goals and assists throughout the season.

- ⚽ KNVB Cup Victory: He also helped Ajax win the KNVB Cup in the 2020-2021 season, adding another trophy to his growing list of achievements.
- ⚽ Champions League Impact: Kudus made his UEFA Champions League debut on 21 October 2020 against Liverpool. He scored four goals in nine appearances in the competition, highlighting his

ability to perform on the big stage.

⚽   Versatility: Kudus is known for his versatility on the pitch, capable of playing as an attacking midfielder, centre-forward, or right winger, providing tactical flexibility for his coaches.

⚽   Transfer to West Ham United: In August 2023, Kudus transferred to Premier League club West Ham

United for a fee that could rise to €46 million (£39.5 million) with add-ons.

- ⚽ **West Ham Debut:** He made his debut for West Ham United on 27 August 2023 in a Premier League match against Brighton & Hove Albion, making an immediate impact.
- ⚽ **First Premier League Goal:** Kudus scored his first Premier League goal on 22 October

2023 in a 2-1 win against Aston Villa, quickly becoming a fan favourite.

- ⚽ High Market Value: As of 2024, Kudus's market value stands at €50 million, reflecting his status as one of the most promising young talents in European football.
- ⚽ Consistent Performance: Throughout his career, Kudus has maintained a consistent performance level,

contributing goals and assists regularly across different leagues and competitions.

- ⚽ Championship Experience: Kudus has participated in various league championship rounds, including the Superliga Championship round with FC Nordsjaelland, where he continued to impress with his performances.

⚽   European Success: Kudus's contributions in the Europa League have been notable, scoring six goals in 14 appearances during his time at Ajax, demonstrating his impact in European competitions.

⚽   Recognition and Awards: Kudus's performances have earned him several individual accolades, including being named one of the most promising young players in Europe and receiving nominations for prestigious awards like the Golden Boy.

NATIONAL TEAM CAREER

- International Debut: Mohammed Kudus made his debut for the Ghana national team on 14 November 2019 in a 2021 Africa Cup of Nations (AFCON) qualifier against South Africa. He scored a goal in the 2-0 victory.
- First International Goal: Kudus scored his first

international goal during his debut match against South Africa, making an immediate impact on the national stage.

⚽ AFCON Participation: Kudus has represented Ghana in multiple Africa Cup of Nations tournaments, including the 2021 edition, where his performances were crucial for the team.

⚽ World Cup Qualification: He played a key role in

Ghana's qualification campaign for the 2022 FIFA World Cup, contributing with goals and assists in crucial matches.

⚽   Versatile Midfielder: Kudus is known for his versatility on the pitch, playing as an attacking midfielder, winger, and sometimes as a centre-forward for the national team.

⚽   Youth National Teams: Before joining the senior

team, Kudus represented Ghana at various youth levels, including the U17 and U20 teams, showcasing his talent from a young age.

⚽   Impact Player: Kudus has often been brought on as a substitute to change the dynamics of the game with his pace, creativity, and goal-scoring ability.

⚽   Key Player for Ghana: Since his debut, Kudus has

become a key player for the Black Stars, often being relied upon in important matches due to his skill and football intelligence.

⚽   Memorable Performances: One of his standout performances came against Zimbabwe in a World Cup qualifier in October 2021, where he scored and assisted, leading Ghana to a 3-1 win.

- ⚽ Injury Setbacks: Despite his talent, Kudus has faced several injury setbacks that have kept him out of important national team fixtures. However, his resilience and determination have seen him bounce back each time.
- ⚽ Goals and Assists: As of 2024, Kudus has scored 11 goals in 34 appearances for the Ghana national team,

highlighting his attacking contributions.

- ⚽ Role Model: Kudus's journey from Nima to the international stage has made him a role model for many young Ghanaian footballers who aspire to represent their country.
- ⚽ Champions League Influence: His performances in the UEFA Champions League with Ajax have

bolstered his reputation, bringing valuable experience to the national team.

- ⚽ Influential Matches: Kudus played a crucial role in Ghana's 1-0 victory over Ethiopia in a World Cup qualifier in September 2021, where he provided the assist for the winning goal.
- ⚽ Adaptability: His ability to adapt to different playing styles and tactical setups has

made him a versatile asset for the national team, capable of fitting into various formations.

- ⚽ Leadership Potential: At a young age, Kudus has shown leadership qualities on the field, often motivating and guiding his teammates during challenging matches.
- ⚽ Copa Africa Experience: Kudus's experience in continental tournaments like the AFCON has been

invaluable for Ghana, providing stability and creativity in midfield.

⚽   High Work Rate: Known for his high work rate and relentless pressing, Kudus contributes significantly to both the defensive and offensive phases of the game.

⚽   Fan Favourite: Kudus's exciting style of play and crucial contributions have made him a favourite among

Ghanaian fans, who admire his talent and dedication.

- ⚽ Future Aspirations: Kudus aims to lead Ghana to further success in international competitions, with dreams of winning the AFCON and making a significant impact in future World Cups.

RECORDS AND PERSONAL ACHIEVEMENTS

⚽ Dutch Eredivisie Champion: Mohammed Kudus won the Eredivisie title twice with Ajax Amsterdam, in the 2020-2021 and 2021-2022 seasons. His contributions in midfield were pivotal to Ajax's domestic dominance.

- ⚽ KNVB Cup Winner: In the 2020-2021 season, Kudus helped Ajax secure the KNVB Cup, showcasing his ability to perform in knockout competitions and contributing to the team's overall success.
- ⚽ World Cup Participant: Kudus represented Ghana in the 2022 FIFA World Cup, scoring two goals in the tournament. His

performances on the world stage highlighted his talent and potential.

- ⚽ Under-17 World Cup: Kudus participated in the 2017 FIFA U-17 World Cup with Ghana, where he scored one goal. This early exposure to international football set the stage for his future successes.
- ⚽ Champions League Impact: Kudus has been a key

player for Ajax in the UEFA Champions League, participating in the 2020-2021, 2021-2022, and 2022-2023 seasons. Notably, he scored four goals in the 2022-2023 campaign, demonstrating his ability to compete at the highest level.

⚽   Europa League Participation: During the 2020-2021 season, Kudus played in the UEFA Europa

League with Ajax. His experience in European competitions has been crucial in his development as a versatile midfielder.

- ⚽ Dutch Cup Runner-Up: In the 2021-2022 season, Kudus and Ajax reached the final of the KNVB Cup but finished as runners-up. Despite the loss, Kudus's performances throughout the tournament were commendable.

- ⚽   Market Value: As of May 2024, Kudus's market value is estimated at €50 million, reflecting his status as one of the most promising young talents in European football.
- ⚽   Consistent Goal Scorer: Throughout his career, Kudus has maintained a consistent goal-scoring record, contributing crucial goals for both club and country. His attacking prowess is a

significant asset to any team he plays for.

- High Work Ethic and Versatility: Kudus's ability to play in multiple positions—attacking midfield, centre-forward, and right winger—along with his high work ethic, has made him an invaluable player for his teams. His versatility allows managers to deploy him in various tactical setups, enhancing team performance.

TECHNIQUE AND PLAYING STYLE

- ⚽ Exceptional Ball Control: Mohammed Kudus is known for his exceptional ball control. His ability to maintain possession under pressure and manoeuvre through tight spaces makes him a formidable player in the attacking midfield role.

⚽   Versatility on the Field: Kudus is a versatile player capable of performing in multiple positions. He can play as an attacking midfielder, centre-forward, or right winger, allowing his managers to deploy him in various tactical setups to exploit different defensive weaknesses.

⚽   Dynamic Dribbling: One of Kudus's standout attributes is his dynamic dribbling. He combines speed with intricate footwork, often leaving defenders in his wake. His dribbling skills make him a constant threat in one-on-one situations.

⚽   Powerful Shooting: Kudus has a powerful and accurate shot, capable of scoring from distance. His ability to strike the ball cleanly with both feet adds a valuable dimension to his attacking play, making him a threat from outside the box.

⚽   Creative Playmaking: Kudus excels in creating scoring opportunities for his teammates. His vision and precise passing allow him to deliver key passes that break through defensive lines, making him an essential playmaker in the final third.

- ⚽ High Work Rate: Kudus is known for his high work rate and relentless energy on the pitch. He constantly presses opponents, chases down loose balls, and contributes defensively, making him a well-rounded midfielder.
- ⚽ Aerial Ability: Despite not being particularly tall, Kudus has a notable aerial presence. His timing and leap allow him to win headers in both

defensive and offensive situations, contributing to set-piece play.

⚽ Spatial Awareness: Kudus possesses excellent spatial awareness, enabling him to position himself effectively to receive passes and exploit gaps in the opposition's defence. This awareness also aids him in making intelligent runs behind the defensive line.

- ⚽   Composure Under Pressure: Kudus remains calm and composed even in high-pressure situations. His ability to make quick decisions and execute precise actions under pressure is a testament to his maturity and football intelligence.
- ⚽   Defensive Contributions: While primarily an attacking player, Kudus does not shy away from his defensive

duties. He often tracks back to support the defence, showing his commitment and understanding of the game's defensive aspects.

Printed in Dunstable, United Kingdom